GCC 5.2 GNU GCJ Reference Manual

A catalogue record for this book is available from the Hong Kong Public Libraries.

Published in Hong Kong by Samurai Media Limited.

Email: info@samuraimedia.org

ISBN 978-988-8381-85-2

Table of Contents

Introduction

This manual describes how to use `gcj`, the GNU compiler for the Java programming language. `gcj` can generate both '`.class`' files and object files, and it can read both Java source code and '`.class`' files.

GNU General Public License

Version 3, 29 June 2007

Copyright © 2007 Free Software Foundation, Inc. http://fsf.org/

Everyone is permitted to copy and distribute verbatim copies of this license document, but changing it is not allowed.

Preamble

The GNU General Public License is a free, copyleft license for software and other kinds of works.

The licenses for most software and other practical works are designed to take away your freedom to share and change the works. By contrast, the GNU General Public License is intended to guarantee your freedom to share and change all versions of a program–to make sure it remains free software for all its users. We, the Free Software Foundation, use the GNU General Public License for most of our software; it applies also to any other work released this way by its authors. You can apply it to your programs, too.

When we speak of free software, we are referring to freedom, not price. Our General Public Licenses are designed to make sure that you have the freedom to distribute copies of free software (and charge for them if you wish), that you receive source code or can get it if you want it, that you can change the software or use pieces of it in new free programs, and that you know you can do these things.

To protect your rights, we need to prevent others from denying you these rights or asking you to surrender the rights. Therefore, you have certain responsibilities if you distribute copies of the software, or if you modify it: responsibilities to respect the freedom of others.

For example, if you distribute copies of such a program, whether gratis or for a fee, you must pass on to the recipients the same freedoms that you received. You must make sure that they, too, receive or can get the source code. And you must show them these terms so they know their rights.

Developers that use the GNU GPL protect your rights with two steps: (1) assert copyright on the software, and (2) offer you this License giving you legal permission to copy, distribute and/or modify it.

For the developers' and authors' protection, the GPL clearly explains that there is no warranty for this free software. For both users' and authors' sake, the GPL requires that modified versions be marked as changed, so that their problems will not be attributed erroneously to authors of previous versions.

Some devices are designed to deny users access to install or run modified versions of the software inside them, although the manufacturer can do so. This is fundamentally incompatible with the aim of protecting users' freedom to change the software. The systematic pattern of such abuse occurs in the area of products for individuals to use, which is precisely where it is most unacceptable. Therefore, we have designed this version of the GPL to prohibit the practice for those products. If such problems arise substantially in other domains, we stand ready to extend this provision to those domains in future versions of the GPL, as needed to protect the freedom of users.

Finally, every program is threatened constantly by software patents. States should not allow patents to restrict development and use of software on general-purpose computers, but in those that do, we wish to avoid the special danger that patents applied to a free program could make it effectively proprietary. To prevent this, the GPL assures that patents cannot be used to render the program non-free.

The precise terms and conditions for copying, distribution and modification follow.

TERMS AND CONDITIONS

0. Definitions.

   "This License" refers to version 3 of the GNU General Public License.

   "Copyright" also means copyright-like laws that apply to other kinds of works, such as semiconductor masks.

   "The Program" refers to any copyrightable work licensed under this License. Each licensee is addressed as "you". "Licensees" and "recipients" may be individuals or organizations.

   To "modify" a work means to copy from or adapt all or part of the work in a fashion requiring copyright permission, other than the making of an exact copy. The resulting work is called a "modified version" of the earlier work or a work "based on" the earlier work.

   A "covered work" means either the unmodified Program or a work based on the Program.

   To "propagate" a work means to do anything with it that, without permission, would make you directly or secondarily liable for infringement under applicable copyright law, except executing it on a computer or modifying a private copy. Propagation includes copying, distribution (with or without modification), making available to the public, and in some countries other activities as well.

   To "convey" a work means any kind of propagation that enables other parties to make or receive copies. Mere interaction with a user through a computer network, with no transfer of a copy, is not conveying.

   An interactive user interface displays "Appropriate Legal Notices" to the extent that it includes a convenient and prominently visible feature that (1) displays an appropriate copyright notice, and (2) tells the user that there is no warranty for the work (except to the extent that warranties are provided), that licensees may convey the work under this License, and how to view a copy of this License. If the interface presents a list of user commands or options, such as a menu, a prominent item in the list meets this criterion.

1. Source Code.

   The "source code" for a work means the preferred form of the work for making modifications to it. "Object code" means any non-source form of a work.

   A "Standard Interface" means an interface that either is an official standard defined by a recognized standards body, or, in the case of interfaces specified for a particular programming language, one that is widely used among developers working in that language.

The "System Libraries" of an executable work include anything, other than the work as a whole, that (a) is included in the normal form of packaging a Major Component, but which is not part of that Major Component, and (b) serves only to enable use of the work with that Major Component, or to implement a Standard Interface for which an implementation is available to the public in source code form. A "Major Component", in this context, means a major essential component (kernel, window system, and so on) of the specific operating system (if any) on which the executable work runs, or a compiler used to produce the work, or an object code interpreter used to run it.

The "Corresponding Source" for a work in object code form means all the source code needed to generate, install, and (for an executable work) run the object code and to modify the work, including scripts to control those activities. However, it does not include the work's System Libraries, or general-purpose tools or generally available free programs which are used unmodified in performing those activities but which are not part of the work. For example, Corresponding Source includes interface definition files associated with source files for the work, and the source code for shared libraries and dynamically linked subprograms that the work is specifically designed to require, such as by intimate data communication or control flow between those subprograms and other parts of the work.

The Corresponding Source need not include anything that users can regenerate automatically from other parts of the Corresponding Source.

The Corresponding Source for a work in source code form is that same work.

2. Basic Permissions.

All rights granted under this License are granted for the term of copyright on the Program, and are irrevocable provided the stated conditions are met. This License explicitly affirms your unlimited permission to run the unmodified Program. The output from running a covered work is covered by this License only if the output, given its content, constitutes a covered work. This License acknowledges your rights of fair use or other equivalent, as provided by copyright law.

You may make, run and propagate covered works that you do not convey, without conditions so long as your license otherwise remains in force. You may convey covered works to others for the sole purpose of having them make modifications exclusively for you, or provide you with facilities for running those works, provided that you comply with the terms of this License in conveying all material for which you do not control copyright. Those thus making or running the covered works for you must do so exclusively on your behalf, under your direction and control, on terms that prohibit them from making any copies of your copyrighted material outside their relationship with you.

Conveying under any other circumstances is permitted solely under the conditions stated below. Sublicensing is not allowed; section 10 makes it unnecessary.

3. Protecting Users' Legal Rights From Anti-Circumvention Law.

No covered work shall be deemed part of an effective technological measure under any applicable law fulfilling obligations under article 11 of the WIPO copyright treaty adopted on 20 December 1996, or similar laws prohibiting or restricting circumvention of such measures.

When you convey a covered work, you waive any legal power to forbid circumvention of technological measures to the extent such circumvention is effected by exercising rights under this License with respect to the covered work, and you disclaim any intention to limit operation or modification of the work as a means of enforcing, against the work's users, your or third parties' legal rights to forbid circumvention of technological measures.

4. Conveying Verbatim Copies.

You may convey verbatim copies of the Program's source code as you receive it, in any medium, provided that you conspicuously and appropriately publish on each copy an appropriate copyright notice; keep intact all notices stating that this License and any non-permissive terms added in accord with section 7 apply to the code; keep intact all notices of the absence of any warranty; and give all recipients a copy of this License along with the Program.

You may charge any price or no price for each copy that you convey, and you may offer support or warranty protection for a fee.

5. Conveying Modified Source Versions.

You may convey a work based on the Program, or the modifications to produce it from the Program, in the form of source code under the terms of section 4, provided that you also meet all of these conditions:

    a. The work must carry prominent notices stating that you modified it, and giving a relevant date.

    b. The work must carry prominent notices stating that it is released under this License and any conditions added under section 7. This requirement modifies the requirement in section 4 to "keep intact all notices".

    c. You must license the entire work, as a whole, under this License to anyone who comes into possession of a copy. This License will therefore apply, along with any applicable section 7 additional terms, to the whole of the work, and all its parts, regardless of how they are packaged. This License gives no permission to license the work in any other way, but it does not invalidate such permission if you have separately received it.

    d. If the work has interactive user interfaces, each must display Appropriate Legal Notices; however, if the Program has interactive interfaces that do not display Appropriate Legal Notices, your work need not make them do so.

A compilation of a covered work with other separate and independent works, which are not by their nature extensions of the covered work, and which are not combined with it such as to form a larger program, in or on a volume of a storage or distribution medium, is called an "aggregate" if the compilation and its resulting copyright are not used to limit the access or legal rights of the compilation's users beyond what the individual works permit. Inclusion of a covered work in an aggregate does not cause this License to apply to the other parts of the aggregate.

6. Conveying Non-Source Forms.

You may convey a covered work in object code form under the terms of sections 4 and 5, provided that you also convey the machine-readable Corresponding Source under the terms of this License, in one of these ways:

a. Convey the object code in, or embodied in, a physical product (including a physical distribution medium), accompanied by the Corresponding Source fixed on a durable physical medium customarily used for software interchange.

b. Convey the object code in, or embodied in, a physical product (including a physical distribution medium), accompanied by a written offer, valid for at least three years and valid for as long as you offer spare parts or customer support for that product model, to give anyone who possesses the object code either (1) a copy of the Corresponding Source for all the software in the product that is covered by this License, on a durable physical medium customarily used for software interchange, for a price no more than your reasonable cost of physically performing this conveying of source, or (2) access to copy the Corresponding Source from a network server at no charge.

c. Convey individual copies of the object code with a copy of the written offer to provide the Corresponding Source. This alternative is allowed only occasionally and noncommercially, and only if you received the object code with such an offer, in accord with subsection 6b.

d. Convey the object code by offering access from a designated place (gratis or for a charge), and offer equivalent access to the Corresponding Source in the same way through the same place at no further charge. You need not require recipients to copy the Corresponding Source along with the object code. If the place to copy the object code is a network server, the Corresponding Source may be on a different server (operated by you or a third party) that supports equivalent copying facilities, provided you maintain clear directions next to the object code saying where to find the Corresponding Source. Regardless of what server hosts the Corresponding Source, you remain obligated to ensure that it is available for as long as needed to satisfy these requirements.

e. Convey the object code using peer-to-peer transmission, provided you inform other peers where the object code and Corresponding Source of the work are being offered to the general public at no charge under subsection 6d.

A separable portion of the object code, whose source code is excluded from the Corresponding Source as a System Library, need not be included in conveying the object code work.

A "User Product" is either (1) a "consumer product", which means any tangible personal property which is normally used for personal, family, or household purposes, or (2) anything designed or sold for incorporation into a dwelling. In determining whether a product is a consumer product, doubtful cases shall be resolved in favor of coverage. For a particular product received by a particular user, "normally used" refers to a typical or common use of that class of product, regardless of the status of the particular user or of the way in which the particular user actually uses, or expects or is expected to use, the product. A product is a consumer product regardless of whether the product has substantial commercial, industrial or non-consumer uses, unless such uses represent the only significant mode of use of the product.

"Installation Information" for a User Product means any methods, procedures, authorization keys, or other information required to install and execute modified versions of a covered work in that User Product from a modified version of its Corresponding Source.

The information must suffice to ensure that the continued functioning of the modified object code is in no case prevented or interfered with solely because modification has been made.

If you convey an object code work under this section in, or with, or specifically for use in, a User Product, and the conveying occurs as part of a transaction in which the right of possession and use of the User Product is transferred to the recipient in perpetuity or for a fixed term (regardless of how the transaction is characterized), the Corresponding Source conveyed under this section must be accompanied by the Installation Information. But this requirement does not apply if neither you nor any third party retains the ability to install modified object code on the User Product (for example, the work has been installed in ROM).

The requirement to provide Installation Information does not include a requirement to continue to provide support service, warranty, or updates for a work that has been modified or installed by the recipient, or for the User Product in which it has been modified or installed. Access to a network may be denied when the modification itself materially and adversely affects the operation of the network or violates the rules and protocols for communication across the network.

Corresponding Source conveyed, and Installation Information provided, in accord with this section must be in a format that is publicly documented (and with an implementation available to the public in source code form), and must require no special password or key for unpacking, reading or copying.

7. Additional Terms.

"Additional permissions" are terms that supplement the terms of this License by making exceptions from one or more of its conditions. Additional permissions that are applicable to the entire Program shall be treated as though they were included in this License, to the extent that they are valid under applicable law. If additional permissions apply only to part of the Program, that part may be used separately under those permissions, but the entire Program remains governed by this License without regard to the additional permissions.

When you convey a copy of a covered work, you may at your option remove any additional permissions from that copy, or from any part of it. (Additional permissions may be written to require their own removal in certain cases when you modify the work.) You may place additional permissions on material, added by you to a covered work, for which you have or can give appropriate copyright permission.

Notwithstanding any other provision of this License, for material you add to a covered work, you may (if authorized by the copyright holders of that material) supplement the terms of this License with terms:

  a. Disclaiming warranty or limiting liability differently from the terms of sections 15 and 16 of this License; or

  b. Requiring preservation of specified reasonable legal notices or author attributions in that material or in the Appropriate Legal Notices displayed by works containing it; or

  c. Prohibiting misrepresentation of the origin of that material, or requiring that modified versions of such material be marked in reasonable ways as different from the original version; or

d. Limiting the use for publicity purposes of names of licensors or authors of the material; or

e. Declining to grant rights under trademark law for use of some trade names, trademarks, or service marks; or

f. Requiring indemnification of licensors and authors of that material by anyone who conveys the material (or modified versions of it) with contractual assumptions of liability to the recipient, for any liability that these contractual assumptions directly impose on those licensors and authors.

All other non-permissive additional terms are considered "further restrictions" within the meaning of section 10. If the Program as you received it, or any part of it, contains a notice stating that it is governed by this License along with a term that is a further restriction, you may remove that term. If a license document contains a further restriction but permits relicensing or conveying under this License, you may add to a covered work material governed by the terms of that license document, provided that the further restriction does not survive such relicensing or conveying.

If you add terms to a covered work in accord with this section, you must place, in the relevant source files, a statement of the additional terms that apply to those files, or a notice indicating where to find the applicable terms.

Additional terms, permissive or non-permissive, may be stated in the form of a separately written license, or stated as exceptions; the above requirements apply either way.

8. Termination.

You may not propagate or modify a covered work except as expressly provided under this License. Any attempt otherwise to propagate or modify it is void, and will automatically terminate your rights under this License (including any patent licenses granted under the third paragraph of section 11).

However, if you cease all violation of this License, then your license from a particular copyright holder is reinstated (a) provisionally, unless and until the copyright holder explicitly and finally terminates your license, and (b) permanently, if the copyright holder fails to notify you of the violation by some reasonable means prior to 60 days after the cessation.

Moreover, your license from a particular copyright holder is reinstated permanently if the copyright holder notifies you of the violation by some reasonable means, this is the first time you have received notice of violation of this License (for any work) from that copyright holder, and you cure the violation prior to 30 days after your receipt of the notice.

Termination of your rights under this section does not terminate the licenses of parties who have received copies or rights from you under this License. If your rights have been terminated and not permanently reinstated, you do not qualify to receive new licenses for the same material under section 10.

9. Acceptance Not Required for Having Copies.

You are not required to accept this License in order to receive or run a copy of the Program. Ancillary propagation of a covered work occurring solely as a consequence of using peer-to-peer transmission to receive a copy likewise does not require acceptance.

However, nothing other than this License grants you permission to propagate or modify any covered work. These actions infringe copyright if you do not accept this License. Therefore, by modifying or propagating a covered work, you indicate your acceptance of this License to do so.

10. Automatic Licensing of Downstream Recipients.

Each time you convey a covered work, the recipient automatically receives a license from the original licensors, to run, modify and propagate that work, subject to this License. You are not responsible for enforcing compliance by third parties with this License.

An "entity transaction" is a transaction transferring control of an organization, or substantially all assets of one, or subdividing an organization, or merging organizations. If propagation of a covered work results from an entity transaction, each party to that transaction who receives a copy of the work also receives whatever licenses to the work the party's predecessor in interest had or could give under the previous paragraph, plus a right to possession of the Corresponding Source of the work from the predecessor in interest, if the predecessor has it or can get it with reasonable efforts.

You may not impose any further restrictions on the exercise of the rights granted or affirmed under this License. For example, you may not impose a license fee, royalty, or other charge for exercise of rights granted under this License, and you may not initiate litigation (including a cross-claim or counterclaim in a lawsuit) alleging that any patent claim is infringed by making, using, selling, offering for sale, or importing the Program or any portion of it.

11. Patents.

A "contributor" is a copyright holder who authorizes use under this License of the Program or a work on which the Program is based. The work thus licensed is called the contributor's "contributor version".

A contributor's "essential patent claims" are all patent claims owned or controlled by the contributor, whether already acquired or hereafter acquired, that would be infringed by some manner, permitted by this License, of making, using, or selling its contributor version, but do not include claims that would be infringed only as a consequence of further modification of the contributor version. For purposes of this definition, "control" includes the right to grant patent sublicenses in a manner consistent with the requirements of this License.

Each contributor grants you a non-exclusive, worldwide, royalty-free patent license under the contributor's essential patent claims, to make, use, sell, offer for sale, import and otherwise run, modify and propagate the contents of its contributor version.

In the following three paragraphs, a "patent license" is any express agreement or commitment, however denominated, not to enforce a patent (such as an express permission to practice a patent or covenant not to sue for patent infringement). To "grant" such a patent license to a party means to make such an agreement or commitment not to enforce a patent against the party.

If you convey a covered work, knowingly relying on a patent license, and the Corresponding Source of the work is not available for anyone to copy, free of charge and under the terms of this License, through a publicly available network server or other readily accessible means, then you must either (1) cause the Corresponding Source to be so available, or (2) arrange to deprive yourself of the benefit of the patent license for this particular work, or (3) arrange, in a manner consistent with the requirements of this License, to extend the patent license to downstream recipients. "Knowingly relying" means you have actual knowledge that, but for the patent license, your conveying the covered work in a country, or your recipient's use of the covered work in a country, would infringe one or more identifiable patents in that country that you have reason to believe are valid.

If, pursuant to or in connection with a single transaction or arrangement, you convey, or propagate by procuring conveyance of, a covered work, and grant a patent license to some of the parties receiving the covered work authorizing them to use, propagate, modify or convey a specific copy of the covered work, then the patent license you grant is automatically extended to all recipients of the covered work and works based on it.

A patent license is "discriminatory" if it does not include within the scope of its coverage, prohibits the exercise of, or is conditioned on the non-exercise of one or more of the rights that are specifically granted under this License. You may not convey a covered work if you are a party to an arrangement with a third party that is in the business of distributing software, under which you make payment to the third party based on the extent of your activity of conveying the work, and under which the third party grants, to any of the parties who would receive the covered work from you, a discriminatory patent license (a) in connection with copies of the covered work conveyed by you (or copies made from those copies), or (b) primarily for and in connection with specific products or compilations that contain the covered work, unless you entered into that arrangement, or that patent license was granted, prior to 28 March 2007.

Nothing in this License shall be construed as excluding or limiting any implied license or other defenses to infringement that may otherwise be available to you under applicable patent law.

12. No Surrender of Others' Freedom.

If conditions are imposed on you (whether by court order, agreement or otherwise) that contradict the conditions of this License, they do not excuse you from the conditions of this License. If you cannot convey a covered work so as to satisfy simultaneously your obligations under this License and any other pertinent obligations, then as a consequence you may not convey it at all. For example, if you agree to terms that obligate you to collect a royalty for further conveying from those to whom you convey the Program, the only way you could satisfy both those terms and this License would be to refrain entirely from conveying the Program.

13. Use with the GNU Affero General Public License.

Notwithstanding any other provision of this License, you have permission to link or combine any covered work with a work licensed under version 3 of the GNU Affero General Public License into a single combined work, and to convey the resulting work. The terms of this License will continue to apply to the part which is the covered work, but the special requirements of the GNU Affero General Public License, section 13, concerning interaction through a network will apply to the combination as such.

14. Revised Versions of this License.

The Free Software Foundation may publish revised and/or new versions of the GNU General Public License from time to time. Such new versions will be similar in spirit to the present version, but may differ in detail to address new problems or concerns.

Each version is given a distinguishing version number. If the Program specifies that a certain numbered version of the GNU General Public License "or any later version" applies to it, you have the option of following the terms and conditions either of that numbered version or of any later version published by the Free Software Foundation. If the Program does not specify a version number of the GNU General Public License, you may choose any version ever published by the Free Software Foundation.

If the Program specifies that a proxy can decide which future versions of the GNU General Public License can be used, that proxy's public statement of acceptance of a version permanently authorizes you to choose that version for the Program.

Later license versions may give you additional or different permissions. However, no additional obligations are imposed on any author or copyright holder as a result of your choosing to follow a later version.

15. Disclaimer of Warranty.

THERE IS NO WARRANTY FOR THE PROGRAM, TO THE EXTENT PERMITTED BY APPLICABLE LAW. EXCEPT WHEN OTHERWISE STATED IN WRITING THE COPYRIGHT HOLDERS AND/OR OTHER PARTIES PROVIDE THE PROGRAM "AS IS" WITHOUT WARRANTY OF ANY KIND, EITHER EXPRESSED OR IMPLIED, INCLUDING, BUT NOT LIMITED TO, THE IMPLIED WARRANTIES OF MERCHANTABILITY AND FITNESS FOR A PARTICULAR PURPOSE. THE ENTIRE RISK AS TO THE QUALITY AND PERFORMANCE OF THE PROGRAM IS WITH YOU. SHOULD THE PROGRAM PROVE DEFECTIVE, YOU ASSUME THE COST OF ALL NECESSARY SERVICING, REPAIR OR CORRECTION.

16. Limitation of Liability.

IN NO EVENT UNLESS REQUIRED BY APPLICABLE LAW OR AGREED TO IN WRITING WILL ANY COPYRIGHT HOLDER, OR ANY OTHER PARTY WHO MODIFIES AND/OR CONVEYS THE PROGRAM AS PERMITTED ABOVE, BE LIABLE TO YOU FOR DAMAGES, INCLUDING ANY GENERAL, SPECIAL, INCIDENTAL OR CONSEQUENTIAL DAMAGES ARISING OUT OF THE USE OR INABILITY TO USE THE PROGRAM (INCLUDING BUT NOT LIMITED TO LOSS OF DATA OR DATA BEING RENDERED INACCURATE OR LOSSES SUSTAINED BY YOU OR THIRD PARTIES OR A FAILURE OF THE PROGRAM TO OPERATE WITH ANY OTHER PROGRAMS), EVEN IF SUCH HOLDER OR OTHER PARTY HAS BEEN ADVISED OF THE POSSIBILITY OF SUCH DAMAGES.

17. Interpretation of Sections 15 and 16.

If the disclaimer of warranty and limitation of liability provided above cannot be given local legal effect according to their terms, reviewing courts shall apply local law that most closely approximates an absolute waiver of all civil liability in connection with the Program, unless a warranty or assumption of liability accompanies a copy of the Program in return for a fee.

END OF TERMS AND CONDITIONS

How to Apply These Terms to Your New Programs

If you develop a new program, and you want it to be of the greatest possible use to the public, the best way to achieve this is to make it free software which everyone can redistribute and change under these terms.

To do so, attach the following notices to the program. It is safest to attach them to the start of each source file to most effectively state the exclusion of warranty; and each file should have at least the "copyright" line and a pointer to where the full notice is found.

```
one line to give the program's name and a brief idea of what it does.
Copyright (C) year name of author

This program is free software: you can redistribute it and/or modify
it under the terms of the GNU General Public License as published by
the Free Software Foundation, either version 3 of the License, or (at
your option) any later version.

This program is distributed in the hope that it will be useful, but
WITHOUT ANY WARRANTY; without even the implied warranty of
MERCHANTABILITY or FITNESS FOR A PARTICULAR PURPOSE.  See the GNU
General Public License for more details.

You should have received a copy of the GNU General Public License
along with this program.  If not, see http://www.gnu.org/licenses/.
```

Also add information on how to contact you by electronic and paper mail.

If the program does terminal interaction, make it output a short notice like this when it starts in an interactive mode:

```
program Copyright (C) year name of author
This program comes with ABSOLUTELY NO WARRANTY; for details type 'show w'.
This is free software, and you are welcome to redistribute it
under certain conditions; type 'show c' for details.
```

The hypothetical commands 'show w' and 'show c' should show the appropriate parts of the General Public License. Of course, your program's commands might be different; for a GUI interface, you would use an "about box".

You should also get your employer (if you work as a programmer) or school, if any, to sign a "copyright disclaimer" for the program, if necessary. For more information on this, and how to apply and follow the GNU GPL, see http://www.gnu.org/licenses/.

The GNU General Public License does not permit incorporating your program into proprietary programs. If your program is a subroutine library, you may consider it more useful to permit linking proprietary applications with the library. If this is what you want to do, use the GNU Lesser General Public License instead of this License. But first, please read http://www.gnu.org/philosophy/why-not-lgpl.html.

GNU Free Documentation License

Version 1.3, 3 November 2008

Copyright © 2000, 2001, 2002, 2007, 2008 Free Software Foundation, Inc.
http://fsf.org/

Everyone is permitted to copy and distribute verbatim copies
of this license document, but changing it is not allowed.

0. PREAMBLE

The purpose of this License is to make a manual, textbook, or other functional and useful document *free* in the sense of freedom: to assure everyone the effective freedom to copy and redistribute it, with or without modifying it, either commercially or non-commercially. Secondarily, this License preserves for the author and publisher a way to get credit for their work, while not being considered responsible for modifications made by others.

This License is a kind of "copyleft", which means that derivative works of the document must themselves be free in the same sense. It complements the GNU General Public License, which is a copyleft license designed for free software.

We have designed this License in order to use it for manuals for free software, because free software needs free documentation: a free program should come with manuals providing the same freedoms that the software does. But this License is not limited to software manuals; it can be used for any textual work, regardless of subject matter or whether it is published as a printed book. We recommend this License principally for works whose purpose is instruction or reference.

1. APPLICABILITY AND DEFINITIONS

This License applies to any manual or other work, in any medium, that contains a notice placed by the copyright holder saying it can be distributed under the terms of this License. Such a notice grants a world-wide, royalty-free license, unlimited in duration, to use that work under the conditions stated herein. The "Document", below, refers to any such manual or work. Any member of the public is a licensee, and is addressed as "you". You accept the license if you copy, modify or distribute the work in a way requiring permission under copyright law.

A "Modified Version" of the Document means any work containing the Document or a portion of it, either copied verbatim, or with modifications and/or translated into another language.

A "Secondary Section" is a named appendix or a front-matter section of the Document that deals exclusively with the relationship of the publishers or authors of the Document to the Document's overall subject (or to related matters) and contains nothing that could fall directly within that overall subject. (Thus, if the Document is in part a textbook of mathematics, a Secondary Section may not explain any mathematics.) The relationship could be a matter of historical connection with the subject or with related matters, or of legal, commercial, philosophical, ethical or political position regarding them.

The "Invariant Sections" are certain Secondary Sections whose titles are designated, as being those of Invariant Sections, in the notice that says that the Document is released under this License. If a section does not fit the above definition of Secondary then it is not allowed to be designated as Invariant. The Document may contain zero Invariant Sections. If the Document does not identify any Invariant Sections then there are none.

The "Cover Texts" are certain short passages of text that are listed, as Front-Cover Texts or Back-Cover Texts, in the notice that says that the Document is released under this License. A Front-Cover Text may be at most 5 words, and a Back-Cover Text may be at most 25 words.

A "Transparent" copy of the Document means a machine-readable copy, represented in a format whose specification is available to the general public, that is suitable for revising the document straightforwardly with generic text editors or (for images composed of pixels) generic paint programs or (for drawings) some widely available drawing editor, and that is suitable for input to text formatters or for automatic translation to a variety of formats suitable for input to text formatters. A copy made in an otherwise Transparent file format whose markup, or absence of markup, has been arranged to thwart or discourage subsequent modification by readers is not Transparent. An image format is not Transparent if used for any substantial amount of text. A copy that is not "Transparent" is called "Opaque".

Examples of suitable formats for Transparent copies include plain ASCII without markup, Texinfo input format, LaTeX input format, SGML or XML using a publicly available DTD, and standard-conforming simple HTML, PostScript or PDF designed for human modification. Examples of transparent image formats include PNG, XCF and JPG. Opaque formats include proprietary formats that can be read and edited only by proprietary word processors, SGML or XML for which the DTD and/or processing tools are not generally available, and the machine-generated HTML, PostScript or PDF produced by some word processors for output purposes only.

The "Title Page" means, for a printed book, the title page itself, plus such following pages as are needed to hold, legibly, the material this License requires to appear in the title page. For works in formats which do not have any title page as such, "Title Page" means the text near the most prominent appearance of the work's title, preceding the beginning of the body of the text.

The "publisher" means any person or entity that distributes copies of the Document to the public.

A section "Entitled XYZ" means a named subunit of the Document whose title either is precisely XYZ or contains XYZ in parentheses following text that translates XYZ in another language. (Here XYZ stands for a specific section name mentioned below, such as "Acknowledgements", "Dedications", "Endorsements", or "History".) To "Preserve the Title" of such a section when you modify the Document means that it remains a section "Entitled XYZ" according to this definition.

The Document may include Warranty Disclaimers next to the notice which states that this License applies to the Document. These Warranty Disclaimers are considered to be included by reference in this License, but only as regards disclaiming warranties: any other implication that these Warranty Disclaimers may have is void and has no effect on the meaning of this License.

2. VERBATIM COPYING

You may copy and distribute the Document in any medium, either commercially or noncommercially, provided that this License, the copyright notices, and the license notice saying this License applies to the Document are reproduced in all copies, and that you add no other conditions whatsoever to those of this License. You may not use technical measures to obstruct or control the reading or further copying of the copies you make or distribute. However, you may accept compensation in exchange for copies. If you distribute a large enough number of copies you must also follow the conditions in section 3.

You may also lend copies, under the same conditions stated above, and you may publicly display copies.

3. COPYING IN QUANTITY

If you publish printed copies (or copies in media that commonly have printed covers) of the Document, numbering more than 100, and the Document's license notice requires Cover Texts, you must enclose the copies in covers that carry, clearly and legibly, all these Cover Texts: Front-Cover Texts on the front cover, and Back-Cover Texts on the back cover. Both covers must also clearly and legibly identify you as the publisher of these copies. The front cover must present the full title with all words of the title equally prominent and visible. You may add other material on the covers in addition. Copying with changes limited to the covers, as long as they preserve the title of the Document and satisfy these conditions, can be treated as verbatim copying in other respects.

If the required texts for either cover are too voluminous to fit legibly, you should put the first ones listed (as many as fit reasonably) on the actual cover, and continue the rest onto adjacent pages.

If you publish or distribute Opaque copies of the Document numbering more than 100, you must either include a machine-readable Transparent copy along with each Opaque copy, or state in or with each Opaque copy a computer-network location from which the general network-using public has access to download using public-standard network protocols a complete Transparent copy of the Document, free of added material. If you use the latter option, you must take reasonably prudent steps, when you begin distribution of Opaque copies in quantity, to ensure that this Transparent copy will remain thus accessible at the stated location until at least one year after the last time you distribute an Opaque copy (directly or through your agents or retailers) of that edition to the public.

It is requested, but not required, that you contact the authors of the Document well before redistributing any large number of copies, to give them a chance to provide you with an updated version of the Document.

4. MODIFICATIONS

You may copy and distribute a Modified Version of the Document under the conditions of sections 2 and 3 above, provided that you release the Modified Version under precisely this License, with the Modified Version filling the role of the Document, thus licensing distribution and modification of the Modified Version to whoever possesses a copy of it. In addition, you must do these things in the Modified Version:

A. Use in the Title Page (and on the covers, if any) a title distinct from that of the Document, and from those of previous versions (which should, if there were any, be listed in the History section of the Document). You may use the same title as a previous version if the original publisher of that version gives permission.

B. List on the Title Page, as authors, one or more persons or entities responsible for authorship of the modifications in the Modified Version, together with at least five of the principal authors of the Document (all of its principal authors, if it has fewer than five), unless they release you from this requirement.

C. State on the Title page the name of the publisher of the Modified Version, as the publisher.

D. Preserve all the copyright notices of the Document.

E. Add an appropriate copyright notice for your modifications adjacent to the other copyright notices.

F. Include, immediately after the copyright notices, a license notice giving the public permission to use the Modified Version under the terms of this License, in the form shown in the Addendum below.

G. Preserve in that license notice the full lists of Invariant Sections and required Cover Texts given in the Document's license notice.

H. Include an unaltered copy of this License.

I. Preserve the section Entitled "History", Preserve its Title, and add to it an item stating at least the title, year, new authors, and publisher of the Modified Version as given on the Title Page. If there is no section Entitled "History" in the Document, create one stating the title, year, authors, and publisher of the Document as given on its Title Page, then add an item describing the Modified Version as stated in the previous sentence.

J. Preserve the network location, if any, given in the Document for public access to a Transparent copy of the Document, and likewise the network locations given in the Document for previous versions it was based on. These may be placed in the "History" section. You may omit a network location for a work that was published at least four years before the Document itself, or if the original publisher of the version it refers to gives permission.

K. For any section Entitled "Acknowledgements" or "Dedications", Preserve the Title of the section, and preserve in the section all the substance and tone of each of the contributor acknowledgements and/or dedications given therein.

L. Preserve all the Invariant Sections of the Document, unaltered in their text and in their titles. Section numbers or the equivalent are not considered part of the section titles.

M. Delete any section Entitled "Endorsements". Such a section may not be included in the Modified Version.

N. Do not retitle any existing section to be Entitled "Endorsements" or to conflict in title with any Invariant Section.

O. Preserve any Warranty Disclaimers.

If the Modified Version includes new front-matter sections or appendices that qualify as Secondary Sections and contain no material copied from the Document, you may at your option designate some or all of these sections as invariant. To do this, add their titles to the list of Invariant Sections in the Modified Version's license notice. These titles must be distinct from any other section titles.

You may add a section Entitled "Endorsements", provided it contains nothing but endorsements of your Modified Version by various parties—for example, statements of peer review or that the text has been approved by an organization as the authoritative definition of a standard.

You may add a passage of up to five words as a Front-Cover Text, and a passage of up to 25 words as a Back-Cover Text, to the end of the list of Cover Texts in the Modified Version. Only one passage of Front-Cover Text and one of Back-Cover Text may be added by (or through arrangements made by) any one entity. If the Document already includes a cover text for the same cover, previously added by you or by arrangement made by the same entity you are acting on behalf of, you may not add another; but you may replace the old one, on explicit permission from the previous publisher that added the old one.

The author(s) and publisher(s) of the Document do not by this License give permission to use their names for publicity for or to assert or imply endorsement of any Modified Version.

5. COMBINING DOCUMENTS

You may combine the Document with other documents released under this License, under the terms defined in section 4 above for modified versions, provided that you include in the combination all of the Invariant Sections of all of the original documents, unmodified, and list them all as Invariant Sections of your combined work in its license notice, and that you preserve all their Warranty Disclaimers.

The combined work need only contain one copy of this License, and multiple identical Invariant Sections may be replaced with a single copy. If there are multiple Invariant Sections with the same name but different contents, make the title of each such section unique by adding at the end of it, in parentheses, the name of the original author or publisher of that section if known, or else a unique number. Make the same adjustment to the section titles in the list of Invariant Sections in the license notice of the combined work.

In the combination, you must combine any sections Entitled "History" in the various original documents, forming one section Entitled "History"; likewise combine any sections Entitled "Acknowledgements", and any sections Entitled "Dedications". You must delete all sections Entitled "Endorsements."

6. COLLECTIONS OF DOCUMENTS

You may make a collection consisting of the Document and other documents released under this License, and replace the individual copies of this License in the various documents with a single copy that is included in the collection, provided that you follow the rules of this License for verbatim copying of each of the documents in all other respects.

You may extract a single document from such a collection, and distribute it individually under this License, provided you insert a copy of this License into the extracted document, and follow this License in all other respects regarding verbatim copying of that document.

7. AGGREGATION WITH INDEPENDENT WORKS

A compilation of the Document or its derivatives with other separate and independent documents or works, in or on a volume of a storage or distribution medium, is called an "aggregate" if the copyright resulting from the compilation is not used to limit the legal rights of the compilation's users beyond what the individual works permit. When the Document is included in an aggregate, this License does not apply to the other works in the aggregate which are not themselves derivative works of the Document.

If the Cover Text requirement of section 3 is applicable to these copies of the Document, then if the Document is less than one half of the entire aggregate, the Document's Cover Texts may be placed on covers that bracket the Document within the aggregate, or the electronic equivalent of covers if the Document is in electronic form. Otherwise they must appear on printed covers that bracket the whole aggregate.

8. TRANSLATION

Translation is considered a kind of modification, so you may distribute translations of the Document under the terms of section 4. Replacing Invariant Sections with translations requires special permission from their copyright holders, but you may include translations of some or all Invariant Sections in addition to the original versions of these Invariant Sections. You may include a translation of this License, and all the license notices in the Document, and any Warranty Disclaimers, provided that you also include the original English version of this License and the original versions of those notices and disclaimers. In case of a disagreement between the translation and the original version of this License or a notice or disclaimer, the original version will prevail.

If a section in the Document is Entitled "Acknowledgements", "Dedications", or "History", the requirement (section 4) to Preserve its Title (section 1) will typically require changing the actual title.

9. TERMINATION

You may not copy, modify, sublicense, or distribute the Document except as expressly provided under this License. Any attempt otherwise to copy, modify, sublicense, or distribute it is void, and will automatically terminate your rights under this License.

However, if you cease all violation of this License, then your license from a particular copyright holder is reinstated (a) provisionally, unless and until the copyright holder explicitly and finally terminates your license, and (b) permanently, if the copyright holder fails to notify you of the violation by some reasonable means prior to 60 days after the cessation.

Moreover, your license from a particular copyright holder is reinstated permanently if the copyright holder notifies you of the violation by some reasonable means, this is the first time you have received notice of violation of this License (for any work) from that copyright holder, and you cure the violation prior to 30 days after your receipt of the notice.

Termination of your rights under this section does not terminate the licenses of parties who have received copies or rights from you under this License. If your rights have been terminated and not permanently reinstated, receipt of a copy of some or all of the same material does not give you any rights to use it.

10. FUTURE REVISIONS OF THIS LICENSE

The Free Software Foundation may publish new, revised versions of the GNU Free Documentation License from time to time. Such new versions will be similar in spirit to the present version, but may differ in detail to address new problems or concerns. See `http://www.gnu.org/copyleft/`.

Each version of the License is given a distinguishing version number. If the Document specifies that a particular numbered version of this License "or any later version" applies to it, you have the option of following the terms and conditions either of that specified version or of any later version that has been published (not as a draft) by the Free Software Foundation. If the Document does not specify a version number of this License, you may choose any version ever published (not as a draft) by the Free Software Foundation. If the Document specifies that a proxy can decide which future versions of this License can be used, that proxy's public statement of acceptance of a version permanently authorizes you to choose that version for the Document.

11. RELICENSING

"Massive Multiauthor Collaboration Site" (or "MMC Site") means any World Wide Web server that publishes copyrightable works and also provides prominent facilities for anybody to edit those works. A public wiki that anybody can edit is an example of such a server. A "Massive Multiauthor Collaboration" (or "MMC") contained in the site means any set of copyrightable works thus published on the MMC site.

"CC-BY-SA" means the Creative Commons Attribution-Share Alike 3.0 license published by Creative Commons Corporation, a not-for-profit corporation with a principal place of business in San Francisco, California, as well as future copyleft versions of that license published by that same organization.

"Incorporate" means to publish or republish a Document, in whole or in part, as part of another Document.

An MMC is "eligible for relicensing" if it is licensed under this License, and if all works that were first published under this License somewhere other than this MMC, and subsequently incorporated in whole or in part into the MMC, (1) had no cover texts or invariant sections, and (2) were thus incorporated prior to November 1, 2008.

The operator of an MMC Site may republish an MMC contained in the site under CC-BY-SA on the same site at any time before August 1, 2009, provided the MMC is eligible for relicensing.

ADDENDUM: How to use this License for your documents

To use this License in a document you have written, include a copy of the License in the document and put the following copyright and license notices just after the title page:

```
Copyright (C)  year  your name.
Permission is granted to copy, distribute and/or modify this document
under the terms of the GNU Free Documentation License, Version 1.3
or any later version published by the Free Software Foundation;
with no Invariant Sections, no Front-Cover Texts, and no Back-Cover
Texts.  A copy of the license is included in the section entitled ``GNU
Free Documentation License''.
```

If you have Invariant Sections, Front-Cover Texts and Back-Cover Texts, replace the "with...Texts." line with this:

```
with the Invariant Sections being list their titles, with
the Front-Cover Texts being list, and with the Back-Cover Texts
being list.
```

If you have Invariant Sections without Cover Texts, or some other combination of the three, merge those two alternatives to suit the situation.

If your document contains nontrivial examples of program code, we recommend releasing these examples in parallel under your choice of free software license, such as the GNU General Public License, to permit their use in free software.

1 Invoking gcj

As gcj is just another front end to gcc, it supports many of the same options as gcc. See Section "Option Summary" in *Using the GNU Compiler Collection (GCC)*. This manual only documents the options specific to gcj.

1.1 Input and output files

A gcj command is like a gcc command, in that it consists of a number of options and file names. The following kinds of input file names are supported:

file.java
> Java source files.

file.class
> Java bytecode files.

file.zip
file.jar   An archive containing one or more .class files, all of which are compiled. The archive may be compressed. Files in an archive which don't end with '.class' are treated as resource files; they are compiled into the resulting object file as 'core:' URLs.

@*file*   A file containing a whitespace-separated list of input file names. (Currently, these must all be .java source files, but that may change.) Each named file is compiled, just as if it had been on the command line.

library.a
library.so
-l*libname*
> Libraries to use when linking. See the gcc manual.

You can specify more than one input file on the gcj command line, in which case they will all be compiled. If you specify a -o *FILENAME* option, all the input files will be compiled together, producing a single output file, named *FILENAME*. This is allowed even when using -S or -c, but not when using -C or --resource. (This is an extension beyond the what plain gcc allows.) (If more than one input file is specified, all must currently be .java files, though we hope to fix this.)

1.2 Input Options

gcj has options to control where it looks to find files it needs. For instance, gcj might need to load a class that is referenced by the file it has been asked to compile. Like other compilers for the Java language, gcj has a notion of a *class path*. There are several options and environment variables which can be used to manipulate the class path. When gcj looks for a given class, it searches the class path looking for matching '.class' or '.java' file. gcj comes with a built-in class path which points at the installed 'libgcj.jar', a file which contains all the standard classes.

In the text below, a directory or path component can refer either to an actual directory on the filesystem, or to a '.zip' or '.jar' file, which gcj will search as if it is a directory.

-I*dir* All directories specified by -I are kept in order and prepended to the class path constructed from all the other options. Unless compatibility with tools like `javac` is important, we recommend always using -I instead of the other options for manipulating the class path.

--classpath=*path*

This sets the class path to *path*, a colon-separated list of paths (on Windows-based systems, a semicolon-separate list of paths). This does not override the builtin ("boot") search path.

--CLASSPATH=*path*

Deprecated synonym for --classpath.

--bootclasspath=*path*

Where to find the standard builtin classes, such as `java.lang.String`.

--extdirs=*path*

For each directory in the *path*, place the contents of that directory at the end of the class path.

CLASSPATH

This is an environment variable which holds a list of paths.

The final class path is constructed like so:

- First come all directories specified via -I.
- If '--classpath' is specified, its value is appended. Otherwise, if the CLASSPATH environment variable is specified, then its value is appended. Otherwise, the current directory (".") is appended.
- If --bootclasspath was specified, append its value. Otherwise, append the built-in system directory, 'libgcj.jar'.
- Finally, if --extdirs was specified, append the contents of the specified directories at the end of the class path. Otherwise, append the contents of the built-in extdirs at `$(prefix)/share/java/ext`.

The classfile built by `gcj` for the class `java.lang.Object` (and placed in `libgcj.jar`) contains a special zero length attribute `gnu.gcj.gcj-compiled`. The compiler looks for this attribute when loading `java.lang.Object` and will report an error if it isn't found, unless it compiles to bytecode (the option -fforce-classes-archive-check can be used to override this behavior in this particular case.)

-fforce-classes-archive-check

This forces the compiler to always check for the special zero length attribute `gnu.gcj.gcj-compiled` in `java.lang.Object` and issue an error if it isn't found.

-fsource=*VERSION*

This option is used to choose the source version accepted by `gcj`. The default is '1.5'.

1.3 Encodings

The Java programming language uses Unicode throughout. In an effort to integrate well with other locales, gcj allows '.java' files to be written using almost any encoding. gcj knows how to convert these encodings into its internal encoding at compile time.

You can use the --encoding=*NAME* option to specify an encoding (of a particular character set) to use for source files. If this is not specified, the default encoding comes from your current locale. If your host system has insufficient locale support, then gcj assumes the default encoding to be the 'UTF-8' encoding of Unicode.

To implement --encoding, gcj simply uses the host platform's iconv conversion routine. This means that in practice gcj is limited by the capabilities of the host platform.

The names allowed for the argument --encoding vary from platform to platform (since they are not standardized anywhere). However, gcj implements the encoding named 'UTF-8' internally, so if you choose to use this for your source files you can be assured that it will work on every host.

1.4 Warnings

gcj implements several warnings. As with other generic gcc warnings, if an option of the form -Wfoo enables a warning, then -Wno-foo will disable it. Here we've chosen to document the form of the warning which will have an effect – the default being the opposite of what is listed.

-Wredundant-modifiers
> With this flag, gcj will warn about redundant modifiers. For instance, it will warn if an interface method is declared public.

-Wextraneous-semicolon
> This causes gcj to warn about empty statements. Empty statements have been deprecated.

-Wno-out-of-date
> This option will cause gcj not to warn when a source file is newer than its matching class file. By default gcj will warn about this.

-Wno-deprecated
> Warn if a deprecated class, method, or field is referred to.

-Wunused   This is the same as gcc's -Wunused.

-Wall   This is the same as -Wredundant-modifiers -Wextraneous-semicolon -Wunused.

1.5 Linking

To turn a Java application into an executable program, you need to link it with the needed libraries, just as for C or C++. The linker by default looks for a global function named main. Since Java does not have global functions, and a collection of Java classes may have more than one class with a main method, you need to let the linker know which of those main methods it should invoke when starting the application. You can do that in any of these ways:

- Specify the class containing the desired **main** method when you link the application, using the **--main** flag, described below.

- Link the Java package(s) into a shared library (dll) rather than an executable. Then invoke the application using the **gij** program, making sure that **gij** can find the libraries it needs.

- Link the Java packages(s) with the flag **-lgij**, which links in the **main** routine from the **gij** command. This allows you to select the class whose **main** method you want to run when you run the application. You can also use other **gij** flags, such as **-D** flags to set properties. Using the **-lgij** library (rather than the **gij** program of the previous mechanism) has some advantages: it is compatible with static linking, and does not require configuring or installing libraries.

These **gij** options relate to linking an executable:

--main=_CLASSNAME_

> This option is used when linking to specify the name of the class whose **main** method should be invoked when the resulting executable is run.

-D_name_**[=**_value_**]**

> This option can only be used with **--main**. It defines a system property named _name_ with value _value_. If _value_ is not specified then it defaults to the empty string. These system properties are initialized at the program's startup and can be retrieved at runtime using the **java.lang.System.getProperty** method.

-lgij   Create an application whose command-line processing is that of the **gij** command.

> This option is an alternative to using **--main**; you cannot use both.

-static-libgcj

> This option causes linking to be done against a static version of the libgcj runtime library. This option is only available if corresponding linker support exists.

> **Caution:** Static linking of libgcj may cause essential parts of libgcj to be omitted. Some parts of libgcj use reflection to load classes at runtime. Since the linker does not see these references at link time, it can omit the referred to classes. The result is usually (but not always) a **ClassNotFoundException** being thrown at runtime. Caution must be used when using this option. For more details see: `http://gcc.gnu.org/wiki/Statically%20linking%20libgcj`

1.6 Code Generation

In addition to the many **gcc** options controlling code generation, **gcj** has several options specific to itself.

-C   This option is used to tell **gcj** to generate bytecode ('**.class**' files) rather than object code.

--resource _resource-name_

> This option is used to tell **gcj** to compile the contents of a given file to object code so it may be accessed at runtime with the core protocol handler

as 'core:/*resource-name*'. Note that *resource-name* is the name of the resource as found at runtime; for instance, it could be used in a call to `ResourceBundle.getBundle`. The actual file name to be compiled this way must be specified separately.

-ftarget=*VERSION*

This can be used with '-C' to choose the version of bytecode emitted by `gcj`. The default is '1.5'. When not generating bytecode, this option has no effect.

-d *directory*

When used with -C, this causes all generated '.class' files to be put in the appropriate subdirectory of *directory*. By default they will be put in subdirectories of the current working directory.

-fno-bounds-check

By default, `gcj` generates code which checks the bounds of all array indexing operations. With this option, these checks are omitted, which can improve performance for code that uses arrays extensively. Note that this can result in unpredictable behavior if the code in question actually does violate array bounds constraints. It is safe to use this option if you are sure that your code will never throw an `ArrayIndexOutOfBoundsException`.

-fno-store-check

Don't generate array store checks. When storing objects into arrays, a runtime check is normally generated in order to ensure that the object is assignment compatible with the component type of the array (which may not be known at compile-time). With this option, these checks are omitted. This can improve performance for code which stores objects into arrays frequently. It is safe to use this option if you are sure your code will never throw an `ArrayStoreException`.

-fjni   With `gcj` there are two options for writing native methods: CNI and JNI. By default `gcj` assumes you are using CNI. If you are compiling a class with native methods, and these methods are implemented using JNI, then you must use -fjni. This option causes `gcj` to generate stubs which will invoke the underlying JNI methods.

-fno-assert

Don't recognize the `assert` keyword. This is for compatibility with older versions of the language specification.

-fno-optimize-static-class-initialization

When the optimization level is greater or equal to -O2, `gcj` will try to optimize the way calls into the runtime are made to initialize static classes upon their first use (this optimization isn't carried out if -C was specified.) When compiling to native code, -fno-optimize-static-class-initialization will turn this optimization off, regardless of the optimization level in use.

--disable-assertions[=*class-or-package*]

Don't include code for checking assertions in the compiled code. If =*class-or-package* is missing disables assertion code generation for all classes, unless overridden by a more specific --enable-assertions flag. If *class-or-package* is a class name, only disables generating assertion checks within the named class or its inner classes. If *class-or-package* is a package name, disables generating assertion checks within the named package or a subpackage.

By default, assertions are enabled when generating class files or when not optimizing, and disabled when generating optimized binaries.

`--enable-assertions`[=*class-or-package*]

Generates code to check assertions. The option is perhaps misnamed, as you still need to turn on assertion checking at run-time, and we don't support any easy way to do that. So this flag isn't very useful yet, except to partially override `--disable-assertions`.

`-findirect-dispatch`

`gcj` has a special binary compatibility ABI, which is enabled by the `-findirect-dispatch` option. In this mode, the code generated by `gcj` honors the binary compatibility guarantees in the Java Language Specification, and the resulting object files do not need to be directly linked against their dependencies. Instead, all dependencies are looked up at runtime. This allows free mixing of interpreted and compiled code.

Note that, at present, `-findirect-dispatch` can only be used when compiling '`.class`' files. It will not work when compiling from source. CNI also does not yet work with the binary compatibility ABI. These restrictions will be lifted in some future release.

However, if you compile CNI code with the standard ABI, you can call it from code built with the binary compatibility ABI.

`-fbootstrap-classes`

This option can be use to tell `libgcj` that the compiled classes should be loaded by the bootstrap loader, not the system class loader. By default, if you compile a class and link it into an executable, it will be treated as if it was loaded using the system class loader. This is convenient, as it means that things like `Class.forName()` will search '`CLASSPATH`' to find the desired class.

`-freduced-reflection`

This option causes the code generated by `gcj` to contain a reduced amount of the class meta-data used to support runtime reflection. The cost of this savings is the loss of the ability to use certain reflection capabilities of the standard Java runtime environment. When set all meta-data except for that which is needed to obtain correct runtime semantics is eliminated.

For code that does not use reflection (i.e. serialization, RMI, CORBA or call methods in the `java.lang.reflect` package), `-freduced-reflection` will result in proper operation with a savings in executable code size.

JNI (`-fjni`) and the binary compatibility ABI (`-findirect-dispatch`) do not work properly without full reflection meta-data. Because of this, it is an error to use these options with `-freduced-reflection`.

Caution: If there is no reflection meta-data, code that uses a `SecurityManager` may not work properly. Also calling `Class.forName()` may fail if the calling method has no reflection meta-data.

1.7 Configure-time Options

Some `gcj` code generations options affect the resulting ABI, and so can only be meaningfully given when `libgcj`, the runtime package, is configured. `libgcj` puts the appropriate options from this group into a 'spec' file which is read by `gcj`. These options are listed here for completeness; if you are using `libgcj` then you won't want to touch these options.

`-fuse-boehm-gc`

>This enables the use of the Boehm GC bitmap marking code. In particular this causes `gcj` to put an object marking descriptor into each vtable.

`-fhash-synchronization`

>By default, synchronization data (the data used for `synchronize`, `wait`, and `notify`) is pointed to by a word in each object. With this option `gcj` assumes that this information is stored in a hash table and not in the object itself.

`-fuse-divide-subroutine`

>On some systems, a library routine is called to perform integer division. This is required to get exception handling correct when dividing by zero.

`-fcheck-references`

>On some systems it's necessary to insert inline checks whenever accessing an object via a reference. On other systems you won't need this because null pointer accesses are caught automatically by the processor.

`-fuse-atomic-builtins`

>On some systems, GCC can generate code for built-in atomic operations. Use this option to force gcj to use these builtins when compiling Java code. Where this capability is present it should be automatically detected, so you won't usually need to use this option.

2 Compatibility with the Java Platform

As we believe it is important that the Java platform not be fragmented, `gcj` and `libgcj` try to conform to the relevant Java specifications. However, limited manpower and incomplete and unclear documentation work against us. So, there are caveats to using `gcj`.

2.1 Standard features not yet supported

This list of compatibility issues is by no means complete.

- `gcj` implements the JDK 1.2 language. It supports inner classes and the new 1.4 **assert** keyword. It does not yet support the Java 2 **strictfp** keyword (it recognizes the keyword but ignores it).

- `libgcj` is largely compatible with the JDK 1.2 libraries. However, `libgcj` is missing many packages, most notably **java.awt**. There are also individual missing classes and methods. We currently do not have a list showing differences between `libgcj` and the Java 2 platform.

- Sometimes the `libgcj` implementation of a method or class differs from the JDK implementation. This is not always a bug. Still, if it affects you, it probably makes sense to report it so that we can discuss the appropriate response.

- `gcj` does not currently allow for piecemeal replacement of components within `libgcj`. Unfortunately, programmers often want to use newer versions of certain packages, such as those provided by the Apache Software Foundation's Jakarta project. This has forced us to place the **org.w3c.dom** and **org.xml.sax** packages into their own libraries, separate from `libgcj`. If you intend to use these classes, you must link them explicitly with **-l-org-w3c-dom** and **-l-org-xml-sax**. Future versions of `gcj` may not have this restriction.

2.2 Extra features unique to gcj

The main feature of `gcj` is that it can compile programs written in the Java programming language to native code. Most extensions that have been added are to facilitate this functionality.

- `gcj` makes it easy and efficient to mix code written in Java and C++. See Chapter 11 [About CNI], page 39, for more info on how to use this in your programs.

- When you compile your classes into a shared library using **-findirect-dispatch** then add them to the system-wide classmap.db file using **gcj-dbtool**, they will be automatically loaded by the `libgcj` system classloader. This is the new, preferred classname-to-library resolution mechanism. See Chapter 5 [Invoking gcj-dbtool], page 33, for more information on using the classmap database.

- The old classname-to-library lookup mechanism is still supported through the **gnu.gcj.runtime.VMClassLoader.library_control** property, but it is deprecated and will likely be removed in some future release. When trying to load a class **gnu.pkg.SomeClass** the system classloader will first try to load the shared library '**lib-gnu-pkg-SomeClass.so**', if that fails to load the class then it will try to load '**lib-gnu-pkg.so**' and finally when the class is still not loaded it will try to load '**lib-gnu.so**'. Note that all '.'s will be transformed into '-'s and that searching for inner classes starts with their outermost outer class. If the class cannot be found this way the system classloader tries to use the `libgcj` bytecode interpreter to load the class from the standard classpath. This process can be controlled to some degree via the `gnu.gcj.runtime.VMClassLoader.library_control` property; See Section 12.3 [libgcj Runtime Properties], page 57.

- `libgcj` includes a special 'gcjlib' URL type. A URL of this form is like a `jar` URL, and looks like 'gcjlib:/path/to/shared/library.so!/path/to/resource'. An access to one of these URLs causes the shared library to be `dlopen()`d, and then the resource is looked for in that library. These URLs are most useful when used in conjunction with `java.net.URLClassLoader`. Note that, due to implementation limitations, currently any such URL can be accessed by only one class loader, and libraries are never unloaded. This means some care must be exercised to make sure that a `gcjlib` URL is not accessed by more than one class loader at once. In a future release this limitation will be lifted, and such libraries will be mapped privately.

- A program compiled by `gcj` will examine the `GCJ_PROPERTIES` environment variable and change its behavior in some ways. In particular `GCJ_PROPERTIES` holds a list of assignments to global properties, such as would be set with the '-D' option to `java`. For instance, 'java.compiler=gcj' is a valid (but currently meaningless) setting.

3 Invoking jcf-dump

This is a class file examiner, similar to `javap`. It will print information about a number of classes, which are specified by class name or file name.

`-c`   Disassemble method bodies. By default method bodies are not printed.

`--print-constants`

        Print the constant pool. When printing a reference to a constant also print its index in the constant pool.

`--javap`   Generate output in `javap` format. The implementation of this feature is very incomplete.

`--classpath=path`
`--CLASSPATH=path`
`-Idirectory`
`-o file`   These options as the same as the corresponding `gcj` options.

`--help`   Print help, then exit.

`--version`

        Print version number, then exit.

`-v, --verbose`

        Print extra information while running. Implies `--print-constants`.

4 Invoking gij

`gij` is a Java bytecode interpreter included with `libgcj`. `gij` is not available on every platform; porting it requires a small amount of assembly programming which has not been done for all the targets supported by `gcj`.

The primary argument to `gij` is the name of a class or, with `-jar`, a jar file. Options before this argument are interpreted by `gij`; remaining options are passed to the interpreted program.

If a class name is specified and this class does not have a `main` method with the appropriate signature (a `static void` method with a `String[]` as its sole argument), then `gij` will print an error and exit.

If a jar file is specified then `gij` will use information in it to determine which class' `main` method will be invoked.

`gij` will invoke the `main` method with all the remaining command-line options.

Note that `gij` is not limited to interpreting code. Because `libgcj` includes a class loader which can dynamically load shared objects, it is possible to give `gij` the name of a class which has been compiled and put into a shared library on the class path.

`-cp` *path*
`-classpath` *path*

> Set the initial class path. The class path is used for finding class and resource files. If specified, this option overrides the `CLASSPATH` environment variable. Note that this option is ignored if `-jar` is used.

`-D`*name*`[=`*value*`]`

> This defines a system property named *name* with value *value*. If *value* is not specified then it defaults to the empty string. These system properties are initialized at the program's startup and can be retrieved at runtime using the `java.lang.System.getProperty` method.

`-ms=`*number*

> Equivalent to `-Xms`.

`-mx=`*number*

> Equivalent to `-Xmx`.

`-noverify`

> Do not verify compliance of bytecode with the VM specification. In addition, this option disables type verification which is otherwise performed on BC-ABI compiled code.

`-X`
`-X`*argument*

> Supplying `-X` by itself will cause `gij` to list all the supported `-X` options. Currently these options are supported:
>
> `-Xms`*size*   Set the initial heap size.
>
> `-Xmx`*size*   Set the maximum heap size.
>
> `-Xss`*size*   Set the thread stack size.

Unrecognized `-X` options are ignored, for compatibility with other runtimes.

`-jar`   This indicates that the name passed to `gij` should be interpreted as the name of a jar file, not a class.

`--help`
`-?`   Print help, then exit.

`--showversion`
Print version number and continue.

`--fullversion`
Print detailed version information, then exit.

`--version`
Print version number, then exit.

`-verbose`
`-verbose:class`
Each time a class is initialized, print a short message on standard error.

`gij` also recognizes and ignores the following options, for compatibility with existing application launch scripts: `-client`, `-server`, `-hotspot`, `-jrockit`, `-agentlib`, `-agentpath`, `-debug`, `-d32`, `-d64`, `-javaagent`, `-noclassgc`, `-verify`, and `-verifyremote`.

5 Invoking gcj-dbtool.

`gcj-dbtool` is a tool for creating and manipulating class file mapping databases. `libgcj` can use these databases to find a shared library corresponding to the bytecode representation of a class. This functionality is useful for ahead-of-time compilation of a program that has no knowledge of `gcj`.

`gcj-dbtool` works best if all the jar files added to it are compiled using `-findirect-dispatch`.

Note that `gcj-dbtool` is currently available as "preview technology". We believe it is a reasonable way to allow application-transparent ahead-of-time compilation, but this is an unexplored area. We welcome your comments.

`-n` *DBFILE* *[SIZE]*

> This creates a new database. Currently, databases cannot be resized; you can choose a larger initial size if desired. The default size is 32,749.

`-a` *DBFILE JARFILE LIB*
`-f` *DBFILE JARFILE LIB*

> This adds a jar file to the database. For each class file in the jar, a cryptographic signature of the bytecode representation of the class is recorded in the database. At runtime, a class is looked up by its signature and the compiled form of the class is looked for in the corresponding shared library. The '`-a`' option will verify that *LIB* exists before adding it to the database; '`-f`' skips this check.

`['-'] ['-0'] -m` *DBFILE DBFILE,[DBFILE]*

> Merge a number of databases. The output database overwrites any existing database. To add databases into an existing database, include the destination in the list of sources.
>
> If '`-`' or '`-0`' are used, the list of files to read is taken from standard input instead of the command line. For '`-0`', Input filenames are terminated by a null character instead of by whitespace. Useful when arguments might contain white space. The GNU find -print0 option produces input suitable for this mode.

`-t` *DBFILE* Test a database.

`-l` *DBFILE* List the contents of a database.

`-p`

> Print the name of the default database. If there is no default database, this prints a blank line. If *LIBDIR* is specified, use it instead of the default library directory component of the database name.

`--help`   Print a help message, then exit.

`--version`
`-v`   Print version information, then exit.

6 Invoking jv-convert

jv-convert ['OPTION'] ... [*INPUTFILE* [*OUTPUTFILE*]]

jv-convert is a utility included with libgcj which converts a file from one encoding to another. It is similar to the Unix iconv utility.

The encodings supported by jv-convert are platform-dependent. Currently there is no way to get a list of all supported encodings.

--encoding *name*
--from *name*
> Use *name* as the input encoding. The default is the current locale's encoding.

--to *name* Use *name* as the output encoding. The default is the JavaSrc encoding; this is ASCII with '\u' escapes for non-ASCII characters.

-i *file*   Read from *file*. The default is to read from standard input.

-o *file*   Write to *file*. The default is to write to standard output.

--reverse
> Swap the input and output encodings.

--help   Print a help message, then exit.

--version
> Print version information, then exit.

7 Invoking grmic

grmic ['OPTION'] ... *class* ...

   grmic is a utility included with libgcj which generates stubs for remote objects.

   Note that this program isn't yet fully compatible with the JDK grmic. Some options, such as '-classpath', are recognized but currently ignored. We have left these options undocumented for now.

   Long options can also be given with a GNU-style leading '--'. For instance, '--help' is accepted.

-keep
-keepgenerated
            By default, grmic deletes intermediate files. Either of these options causes it
            not to delete such files.

-v1.1   Cause grmic to create stubs and skeletons for the 1.1 protocol version.

-vcompat   Cause grmic to create stubs and skeletons compatible with both the 1.1 and
            1.2 protocol versions. This is the default.

-v1.2   Cause grmic to create stubs and skeletons for the 1.2 protocol version.

-nocompile
            Don't compile the generated files.

-verbose   Print information about what grmic is doing.

-d *directory*
            Put output files in *directory*. By default the files are put in the current working
            directory.

-help   Print a help message, then exit.

-version   Print version information, then exit.

8 Invoking gc-analyze

gc-analyze ['OPTION'] ... [*file*]

gc-analyze prints an analysis of a GC memory dump to standard out.

The memory dumps may be created by calling gnu.gcj.util.GCInfo.enumerate(String namePrefix) from java code. A memory dump will be created on an out of memory condition if gnu.gcj.util.GCInfo.setOOMDump(String namePrefix) is called before the out of memory occurs.

Running this program will create two files: 'TestDump001' and 'TestDump001.bytes'.

```
import gnu.gcj.util.*;
import java.util.*;

public class GCDumpTest
{
    static public void main(String args[])
    {
        ArrayList<String> l = new ArrayList<String>(1000);

        for (int i = 1; i < 1500; i++) {
            l.add("This is string #" + i);
        }
        GCInfo.enumerate("TestDump");
    }
}
```

The memory dump may then be displayed by running:

```
gc-analyze -v TestDump001
```

--verbose

-v   Verbose output.

-p *tool-prefix*

Prefix added to the names of the nm and readelf commands.

-d *directory*

Directory that contains the executable and shared libraries used when the dump was generated.

--help   Print a help message, then exit.

--version

Print version information, then exit.

9 Invoking aot-compile

`aot-compile` is a script that searches a directory for Java bytecode (as class files, or in jars) and uses `gcj` to compile it to native code and generate the databases from it.

-M, --make=*PATH*
>   Specify the path to the `make` executable to use.

-C, --gcj=*PATH*
>   Specify the path to the `gcj` executable to use.

-D, --dbtool=*PATH*
>   Specify the path to the `gcj-dbtool` executable to use.

-m, --makeflags=*FLAGS*
>   Specify flags to pass to `make` during the build.

-c, --gcjflags=*FLAGS*
>   Specify flags to pass to `gcj` during compilation, in addition to '-fPIC -findirect-dispatch -fjni'.

-l, --ldflags=*FLAGS*
>   Specify flags to pass to `gcj` during linking, in addition to '-Wl,-Bsymbolic'.

-e, --exclude=*PATH*
>   Do not compile *PATH*.

10 Invoking rebuild-gcj-db

`rebuild-gcj-db` is a script that merges the per-solib databases made by `aot-compile` into one system-wide database so `gij` can find the solibs.

11 About CNI

This documents CNI, the Compiled Native Interface, which is is a convenient way to write Java native methods using C++. This is a more efficient, more convenient, but less portable alternative to the standard JNI (Java Native Interface).

11.1 Basic concepts

In terms of languages features, Java is mostly a subset of C++. Java has a few important extensions, plus a powerful standard class library, but on the whole that does not change the basic similarity. Java is a hybrid object-oriented language, with a few native types, in addition to class types. It is class-based, where a class may have static as well as per-object fields, and static as well as instance methods. Non-static methods may be virtual, and may be overloaded. Overloading is resolved at compile time by matching the actual argument types against the parameter types. Virtual methods are implemented using indirect calls through a dispatch table (virtual function table). Objects are allocated on the heap, and initialized using a constructor method. Classes are organized in a package hierarchy.

All of the listed attributes are also true of C++, though C++ has extra features (for example in C++ objects may be allocated not just on the heap, but also statically or in a local stack frame). Because `gcj` uses the same compiler technology as G++ (the GNU C++ compiler), it is possible to make the intersection of the two languages use the same ABI (object representation and calling conventions). The key idea in CNI is that Java objects are C++ objects, and all Java classes are C++ classes (but not the other way around). So the most important task in integrating Java and C++ is to remove gratuitous incompatibilities.

You write CNI code as a regular C++ source file. (You do have to use a Java/CNI-aware C++ compiler, specifically a recent version of G++.)

A CNI C++ source file must have:

```
#include <gcj/cni.h>
```

and then must include one header file for each Java class it uses, e.g.:

```
#include <java/lang/Character.h>
#include <java/util/Date.h>
#include <java/lang/IndexOutOfBoundsException.h>
```

These header files are automatically generated by `gcjh`.

CNI provides some functions and macros to make using Java objects and primitive types from C++ easier. In general, these CNI functions and macros start with the `Jv` prefix, for example the function `JvNewObjectArray`. This convention is used to avoid conflicts with other libraries. Internal functions in CNI start with the prefix `_Jv_`. You should not call these; if you find a need to, let us know and we will try to come up with an alternate solution.

11.1.1 Limitations

Whilst a Java class is just a C++ class that doesn't mean that you are freed from the shackles of Java, a CNI C++ class must adhere to the rules of the Java programming language.

For example: it is not possible to declare a method in a CNI class that will take a C string (`char*`) as an argument, or to declare a member variable of some non-Java datatype.

11.2 Packages

The only global names in Java are class names, and packages. A *package* can contain zero or more classes, and also zero or more sub-packages. Every class belongs to either an unnamed package or a package that has a hierarchical and globally unique name.

A Java package is mapped to a C++ *namespace*. The Java class `java.lang.String` is in the package `java.lang`, which is a sub-package of `java`. The C++ equivalent is the class `java::lang::String`, which is in the namespace `java::lang` which is in the namespace `java`.

Here is how you could express this:

```
(// Declare the class(es), possibly in a header file:
namespace java {
  namespace lang {
    class Object;
    class String;
    ...
  }
}

class java::lang::String : public java::lang::Object
{
  ...
};
```

The `gcjh` tool automatically generates the necessary namespace declarations.

11.2.1 Leaving out package names

Always using the fully-qualified name of a java class can be tiresomely verbose. Using the full qualified name also ties the code to a single package making code changes necessary should the class move from one package to another. The Java **package** declaration specifies that the following class declarations are in the named package, without having to explicitly name the full package qualifiers. The **package** declaration can be followed by zero or more **import** declarations, which allows either a single class or all the classes in a package to be named by a simple identifier. C++ provides something similar with the **using** declaration and directive.

In Java:

```
import package-name.class-name;
```

allows the program text to refer to *class-name* as a shorthand for the fully qualified name: *package-name.class-name*.

To achieve the same effect C++, you have to do this:

```
using package-name::class-name;
```

Java can also cause imports on demand, like this:

```
import package-name.*;
```

Doing this allows any class from the package *package-name* to be referred to only by its class-name within the program text.

The same effect can be achieved in C++ like this:

```
using namespace package-name;
```

11.3 Primitive types

Java provides 8 *primitives* types which represent integers, floats, characters and booleans (and also the void type). C++ has its own very similar concrete types. Such types in C++ however are not always implemented in the same way (an int might be 16, 32 or 64 bits for example) so CNI provides a special C++ type for each primitive Java type:

Java type	C/C++ typename	Description
char	jchar	16 bit Unicode character
boolean	jboolean	logical (true or false) values
byte	jbyte	8-bit signed integer
short	jshort	16 bit signed integer
int	jint	32 bit signed integer
long	jlong	64 bit signed integer
float	jfloat	32 bit IEEE floating point number
double	jdouble	64 bit IEEE floating point number
void	void	no value

When referring to a Java type You should always use these C++ typenames (e.g.: jint) to avoid disappointment.

11.3.1 Reference types associated with primitive types

In Java each primitive type has an associated reference type, e.g.: boolean has an associated java.lang.Boolean.TYPE class. In order to make working with such classes easier GCJ provides the macro JvPrimClass:

JvPrimClass *type*   [macro]

> Return a pointer to the Class object corresponding to the type supplied.
>
> JvPrimClass(void) ⇒ java.lang.Void.TYPE

11.4 Reference types

A Java reference type is treated as a class in C++. Classes and interfaces are handled this way. A Java reference is translated to a C++ pointer, so for instance a Java java.lang.String becomes, in C++, java::lang::String *.

CNI provides a few built-in typedefs for the most common classes:

Java type	C++ typename	Description
java.lang.Object	jobject	Object type
java.lang.String	jstring	String type
java.lang.Class	jclass	Class type

Every Java class or interface has a corresponding Class instance. These can be accessed in CNI via the static class$ field of a class. The class$ field is of type Class (and not Class *), so you will typically take the address of it.

Here is how you can refer to the class of String, which in Java would be written String.class:

```
using namespace java::lang;
doSomething (&String::class$);
```

11.5 Interfaces

A Java class can *implement* zero or more *interfaces*, in addition to inheriting from a single base class.

CNI allows CNI code to implement methods of interfaces. You can also call methods through interface references, with some limitations.

CNI doesn't understand interface inheritance at all yet. So, you can only call an interface method when the declared type of the field being called matches the interface which declares that method. The workaround is to cast the interface reference to the right superinterface.

For example if you have:

```
interface A
{
  void a();
}

interface B extends A
{
  void b();
}
```

and declare a variable of type B in C++, you can't call a() unless you cast it to an A first.

11.6 Objects and Classes

11.6.1 Classes

All Java classes are derived from `java.lang.Object`. C++ does not have a unique root class, but we use the C++ class `java::lang::Object` as the C++ version of the `java.lang.Object` Java class. All other Java classes are mapped into corresponding C++ classes derived from `java::lang::Object`.

Interface inheritance (the `implements` keyword) is currently not reflected in the C++ mapping.

11.6.2 Object fields

Each object contains an object header, followed by the instance fields of the class, in order. The object header consists of a single pointer to a dispatch or virtual function table. (There may be extra fields *in front of* the object, for example for memory management, but this is invisible to the application, and the reference to the object points to the dispatch table pointer.)

The fields are laid out in the same order, alignment, and size as in C++. Specifically, 8-bit and 16-bit native types (`byte`, `short`, `char`, and `boolean`) are *not* widened to 32 bits. Note that the Java VM does extend 8-bit and 16-bit types to 32 bits when on the VM stack or temporary registers.

If you include the `gcjh`-generated header for a class, you can access fields of Java classes in the *natural* way. For example, given the following Java class:

```
public class Int
{
```

```
    public int i;
    public Int (int i) { this.i = i; }
    public static Int zero = new Int(0);
}
```

you can write:

```
#include <gcj/cni.h>;
#include <Int>;

Int*
mult (Int *p, jint k)
{
  if (k == 0)
    return Int::zero;   // Static member access.
  return new Int(p->i * k);
}
```

11.6.3 Access specifiers

CNI does not strictly enforce the Java access specifiers, because Java permissions cannot be directly mapped into C++ permission. Private Java fields and methods are mapped to private C++ fields and methods, but other fields and methods are mapped to public fields and methods.

11.7 Class Initialization

Java requires that each class be automatically initialized at the time of the first active use. Initializing a class involves initializing the static fields, running code in class initializer methods, and initializing base classes. There may also be some implementation specific actions, such as allocating **String** objects corresponding to string literals in the code.

The GCJ compiler inserts calls to **JvInitClass** at appropriate places to ensure that a class is initialized when required. The C++ compiler does not insert these calls automatically—it is the programmer's responsibility to make sure classes are initialized. However, this is fairly painless because of the conventions assumed by the Java system.

First, **libgcj** will make sure a class is initialized before an instance of that object is created. This is one of the responsibilities of the **new** operation. This is taken care of both in Java code, and in C++ code. When G++ sees a **new** of a Java class, it will call a routine in **libgcj** to allocate the object, and that routine will take care of initializing the class. Note however that this does not happen for Java arrays; you must allocate those using the appropriate CNI function. It follows that you can access an instance field, or call an instance (non-static) method and be safe in the knowledge that the class and all of its base classes have been initialized.

Invoking a static method is also safe. This is because the Java compiler adds code to the start of a static method to make sure the class is initialized. However, the C++ compiler does not add this extra code. Hence, if you write a native static method using CNI, you are responsible for calling **JvInitClass** before doing anything else in the method (unless you are sure it is safe to leave it out).

Accessing a static field also requires the class of the field to be initialized. The Java compiler will generate code to call `JvInitClass` before getting or setting the field. However, the C++ compiler will not generate this extra code, so it is your responsibility to make sure the class is initialized before you access a static field from C++.

11.8 Object allocation

New Java objects are allocated using a *class instance creation expression*, e.g.:

```
new Type ( ... )
```

The same syntax is used in C++. The main difference is that C++ objects have to be explicitly deleted; in Java they are automatically deleted by the garbage collector. Using CNI, you can allocate a new Java object using standard C++ syntax and the C++ compiler will allocate memory from the garbage collector. If you have overloaded constructors, the compiler will choose the correct one using standard C++ overload resolution rules.

For example:

```
java::util::Hashtable *ht = new java::util::Hashtable(120);
```

11.9 Memory allocation

When allocating memory in CNI methods it is best to handle out-of-memory conditions by throwing a Java exception. These functions are provided for that purpose:

void* JvMalloc (*jsize size*)   [Function]
> Calls malloc. Throws `java.lang.OutOfMemoryError` if allocation fails.

void* JvRealloc (*void* ptr*, *jsize size*)   [Function]
> Calls realloc. Throws `java.lang.OutOfMemoryError` if reallocation fails.

void JvFree (*void* ptr*)   [Function]
> Calls free.

11.10 Arrays

While in many ways Java is similar to C and C++, it is quite different in its treatment of arrays. C arrays are based on the idea of pointer arithmetic, which would be incompatible with Java's security requirements. Java arrays are true objects (array types inherit from `java.lang.Object`). An array-valued variable is one that contains a reference (pointer) to an array object.

Referencing a Java array in C++ code is done using the `JArray` template, which as defined as follows:

```
class __JArray : public java::lang::Object
{
public:
  int length;
};

template<class T>
class JArray : public __JArray
```

```
{
  T data[0];
public:
  T& operator[](jint i) { return data[i]; }
};
```

There are a number of **typedefs** which correspond to **typedefs** from the JNI. Each is the type of an array holding objects of the relevant type:

```
typedef __JArray *jarray;
typedef JArray<jobject> *jobjectArray;
typedef JArray<jboolean> *jbooleanArray;
typedef JArray<jbyte> *jbyteArray;
typedef JArray<jchar> *jcharArray;
typedef JArray<jshort> *jshortArray;
typedef JArray<jint> *jintArray;
typedef JArray<jlong> *jlongArray;
typedef JArray<jfloat> *jfloatArray;
typedef JArray<jdouble> *jdoubleArray;
```

T* elements (*JArray<T>* **array**)   [Method on **template<class T>**]

This template function can be used to get a pointer to the elements of the **array**. For instance, you can fetch a pointer to the integers that make up an **int[]** like so:

```
extern jintArray foo;
jint *intp = elements (foo);
```

The name of this function may change in the future.

jobjectArray JvNewObjectArray (*jsize* **length**, *jclass* **klass**, *jobject*   [Function]
     init)

This creates a new array whose elements have reference type. **klass** is the type of elements of the array and **init** is the initial value put into every slot in the array.

```
using namespace java::lang;
JArray<String *> *array
  = (JArray<String *> *) JvNewObjectArray(length, &String::class$, NULL);█
```

11.10.1 Creating arrays

For each primitive type there is a function which can be used to create a new array of that type. The name of the function is of the form:

```
JvNewTypeArray
```

For example:

```
JvNewBooleanArray
```

can be used to create an array of Java primitive boolean types.

The following function definition is the template for all such functions:

jbooleanArray JvNewBooleanArray (*jint* **length**)   [Function]

Creates an array *length* indices long.

jsize JvGetArrayLength (*jarray* **array**)   [Function]

Returns the length of the *array*.

11.11 Methods

Java methods are mapped directly into C++ methods. The header files generated by `gcjh` include the appropriate method definitions. Basically, the generated methods have the same names and *corresponding* types as the Java methods, and are called in the natural manner.

11.11.1 Overloading

Both Java and C++ provide method overloading, where multiple methods in a class have the same name, and the correct one is chosen (at compile time) depending on the argument types. The rules for choosing the correct method are (as expected) more complicated in C++ than in Java, but given a set of overloaded methods generated by `gcjh` the C++ compiler will choose the expected one.

Common assemblers and linkers are not aware of C++ overloading, so the standard implementation strategy is to encode the parameter types of a method into its assembly-level name. This encoding is called *mangling*, and the encoded name is the *mangled name*. The same mechanism is used to implement Java overloading. For C++/Java interoperability, it is important that both the Java and C++ compilers use the *same* encoding scheme.

11.11.2 Static methods

Static Java methods are invoked in CNI using the standard C++ syntax, using the : : operator rather than the . operator.

For example:

```
jint i = java::lang::Math::round((jfloat) 2.3);
```

C++ method definition syntax is used to define a static native method. For example:

```
#include <java/lang/Integer>
java::lang::Integer*
java::lang::Integer::getInteger(jstring str)
{
  ...
}
```

11.11.3 Object Constructors

Constructors are called implicitly as part of object allocation using the **new** operator.

For example:

```
java::lang::Integer *x = new java::lang::Integer(234);
```

Java does not allow a constructor to be a native method. This limitation can be coded round however because a constructor can *call* a native method.

11.11.4 Instance methods

Calling a Java instance method from a C++ CNI method is done using the standard C++ syntax, e.g.:

```
// First create the Java object.
java::lang::Integer *x = new java::lang::Integer(234);
// Now call a method.
jint prim_value = x->intValue();
```

```
if (x->longValue == 0)
    ...
```

Defining a Java native instance method is also done the natural way:

```
#include <java/lang/Integer.h>

jdouble
java::lang:Integer::doubleValue()
{
  return (jdouble) value;
}
```

11.11.5 Interface methods

In Java you can call a method using an interface reference. This is supported, but not completely. See Section 11.5 [Interfaces], page 42.

11.12 Strings

CNI provides a number of utility functions for working with Java Java **String** objects. The names and interfaces are analogous to those of JNI.

jstring JvNewString (*const jchar** **chars**, *jsize* **len**)   [Function]
    Returns a Java **String** object with characters from the array of Unicode characters *chars* up to the index *len* in that array.

jstring JvNewStringLatin1 (*const char** **bytes**, *jsize* **len**)   [Function]
    Returns a Java **String** made up of *len* bytes from *bytes*.

jstring JvNewStringLatin1 (*const char** **bytes**)   [Function]
    As above but the length of the **String** is strlen(*bytes*).

jstring JvNewStringUTF (*const char** **bytes**)   [Function]
    Returns a **String** which is made up of the UTF encoded characters present in the C string *bytes*.

jchar* JvGetStringChars (*jstring* **str**)   [Function]
    Returns a pointer to an array of characters making up the **String** *str*.

int JvGetStringUTFLength (*jstring* **str**)   [Function]
    Returns the number of bytes required to encode the contents of the **String** *str* in UTF-8.

jsize JvGetStringUTFRegion (*jstring* **str**, *jsize* **start**, *jsize* **len**,   [Function]
        char* **buf**)
    Puts the UTF-8 encoding of a region of the **String** *str* into the buffer **buf**. The region to fetch is marked by *start* and *len*.

    Note that *buf* is a buffer, not a C string. It is *not* null terminated.

11.13 Interoperating with C/C++

Because CNI is designed to represent Java classes and methods it cannot be mixed readily with C/C++ types.

One important restriction is that Java classes cannot have non-Java type instance or static variables and cannot have methods which take non-Java types as arguments or return non-Java types.

None of the following is possible with CNI:

```
class ::MyClass : public java::lang::Object
{
    char* variable;   // char* is not a valid Java type.
}
```

```
uint
::SomeClass::someMethod (char *arg)
{

    .

    .

    .

}    // uint is not a valid Java type, neither is char*
```

Of course, it is ok to use C/C++ types within the scope of a method:

```
jint
::SomeClass::otherMethod (jstring str)
{
    char *arg = ...

    .

    .

    .

}
```

11.13.1 RawData

The above restriction can be problematic, so CNI includes the gnu.gcj.RawData class. The RawData class is a *non-scanned reference* type. In other words variables declared of type RawData can contain any data and are not checked by the compiler or memory manager in any way.

This means that you can put C/C++ data structures (including classes) in your CNI classes, as long as you use the appropriate cast.

Here are some examples:

```
class ::MyClass : public java::lang::Object
{
    gnu.gcj.RawData string;
```

```
    MyClass ();
    gnu.gcj.RawData getText ();
    void printText ();
}

::MyClass::MyClass ()
{
    char* text = ...
    string = text;
}

gnu.gcj.RawData
::MyClass::getText ()
{
    return string;
}

void
::MyClass::printText ()
{
    printf("%s\n", (char*) string);
}
```

11.13.2 RawDataManaged

`gnu.gcj.RawDataManaged` is another type used to indicate special data used by native code. Unlike the `RawData` type, fields declared as `RawDataManaged` will be "marked" by the memory manager and considered for garbage collection.

Native data which is allocated using CNI's `JvAllocBytes()` function and stored in a `RawDataManaged` will be automatically freed when the Java object it is associated with becomes unreachable.

11.13.3 Native memory allocation

void* JvAllocBytes (*jsize size*)   [Function]

> Allocates *size* bytes from the heap. The memory returned is zeroed. This memory is not scanned for pointers by the garbage collector, but will be freed if no references to it are discovered.
>
> This function can be useful if you need to associate some native data with a Java object. Using a CNI's special `RawDataManaged` type, native data allocated with `JvAllocBytes` will be automatically freed when the Java object itself becomes unreachable.

11.13.4 Posix signals

On Posix based systems the `libgcj` library uses several signals internally. CNI code should not attempt to use the same signals as doing so may cause `libgcj` and/or the CNI code to fail.

SIGSEGV is used on many systems to generate `NullPointerExceptions`. SIGCHLD is used internally by `Runtime.exec()`. Several other signals (that vary from platform to platform) can be used by the memory manager and by `Thread.interrupt()`.

11.14 Exception Handling

While C++ and Java share a common exception handling framework, things are not yet perfectly integrated. The main issue is that the run-time type information facilities of the two languages are not integrated.

Still, things work fairly well. You can throw a Java exception from C++ using the ordinary `throw` construct, and this exception can be caught by Java code. Similarly, you can catch an exception thrown from Java using the C++ `catch` construct.

Here is an example:

```
if (i >= count)
    throw new java::lang::IndexOutOfBoundsException();
```

Normally, G++ will automatically detect when you are writing C++ code that uses Java exceptions, and handle them appropriately. However, if C++ code only needs to execute destructors when Java exceptions are thrown through it, GCC will guess incorrectly. Sample problematic code:

```
struct S { ~S(); };

extern void bar();      // Is implemented in Java and may throw exceptions.

void foo()
{
  S s;
  bar();
}
```

The usual effect of an incorrect guess is a link failure, complaining of a missing routine called `__gxx_personality_v0`.

You can inform the compiler that Java exceptions are to be used in a translation unit, irrespective of what it might think, by writing `#pragma GCC java_exceptions` at the head of the file. This `#pragma` must appear before any functions that throw or catch exceptions, or run destructors when exceptions are thrown through them.

11.15 Synchronization

Each Java object has an implicit monitor. The Java VM uses the instruction `monitorenter` to acquire and lock a monitor, and `monitorexit` to release it.

The corresponding CNI macros are `JvMonitorEnter` and `JvMonitorExit` (JNI has similar methods `MonitorEnter` and `MonitorExit`).

The Java source language does not provide direct access to these primitives. Instead, there is a `synchronized` statement that does an implicit `monitorenter` before entry to the block, and does a `monitorexit` on exit from the block. Note that the lock has to be released even when the block is abnormally terminated by an exception, which means there is an implicit `try finally` surrounding synchronization locks.

From C++, it makes sense to use a destructor to release a lock. CNI defines the following utility class:

```
class JvSynchronize() {
  jobject obj;
  JvSynchronize(jobject o) { obj = o; JvMonitorEnter(o); }
  ~JvSynchronize() { JvMonitorExit(obj); }
};
```

So this Java code:

```
synchronized (OBJ)
{
    CODE
}
```

might become this C++ code:

```
{
    JvSynchronize dummy (OBJ);
    CODE;
}
```

Java also has methods with the `synchronized` attribute. This is equivalent to wrapping the entire method body in a `synchronized` statement. (Alternatively, an implementation could require the caller to do the synchronization. This is not practical for a compiler, because each virtual method call would have to test at run-time if synchronization is needed.) Since in `gcj` the `synchronized` attribute is handled by the method implementation, it is up to the programmer of a synchronized native method to handle the synchronization (in the C++ implementation of the method). In other words, you need to manually add `JvSynchronize` in a `native synchronized` method.

11.16 Invocation

CNI permits C++ applications to make calls into Java classes, in addition to allowing Java code to call into C++. Several functions, known as the *invocation API*, are provided to support this.

jint JvCreateJavaVM (*JvVMInitArgs** **vm_args**)   [Function]

> Initializes the Java runtime. This function performs essential initialization of the threads interface, garbage collector, exception handling and other key aspects of the runtime. It must be called once by an application with a non-Java `main()` function, before any other Java or CNI calls are made. It is safe, but not recommended, to call `JvCreateJavaVM()` more than once provided it is only called from a single thread. The *vmargs* parameter can be used to specify initialization parameters for the Java runtime. It may be `NULL`.

> JvVMInitArgs represents a list of virtual machine initialization arguments. `JvCreateJavaVM()` ignores the version field.

```
        typedef struct JvVMOption
        {
          // a VM initialization option
          char* optionString;
```

```
      // extra information associated with this option
      void* extraInfo;
    } JvVMOption;

    typedef struct JvVMInitArgs
    {
      // for compatibility with JavaVMInitArgs
      jint version;

      // number of VM initialization options
      jint nOptions;

      // an array of VM initialization options
      JvVMOption* options;

      // true if the option parser should ignore unrecognized options
      jboolean ignoreUnrecognized;
    } JvVMInitArgs;
```

`JvCreateJavaVM()` returns 0 upon success, or −1 if the runtime is already initialized.

Note: In GCJ 3.1, the `vm_args` parameter is ignored. It is recognized and used as of release 4.0.

`java::lang::Thread* JvAttachCurrentThread` (*jstring* **name**,   [Function]
      java::lang::ThreadGroup* **group**)

Registers an existing thread with the Java runtime. This must be called once from each thread, before that thread makes any other Java or CNI calls. It must be called after `JvCreateJavaVM`. *name* specifies a name for the thread. It may be `NULL`, in which case a name will be generated. *group* is the ThreadGroup in which this thread will be a member. If it is `NULL`, the thread will be a member of the main thread group. The return value is the Java `Thread` object that represents the thread. It is safe to call `JvAttachCurrentThread()` more than once from the same thread. If the thread is already attached, the call is ignored and the current thread object is returned.

`jint JvDetachCurrentThread ()`   [Function]

Unregisters a thread from the Java runtime. This should be called by threads that were attached using `JvAttachCurrentThread()`, after they have finished making calls to Java code. This ensures that any resources associated with the thread become eligible for garbage collection. This function returns 0 upon success, or −1 if the current thread is not attached.

11.16.1 Handling uncaught exceptions

If an exception is thrown from Java code called using the invocation API, and no handler for the exception can be found, the runtime will abort the application. In order to make the application more robust, it is recommended that code which uses the invocation API be wrapped by a top-level try/catch block that catches all Java exceptions.

11.16.2 Example

The following code demonstrates the use of the invocation API. In this example, the C++ application initializes the Java runtime and attaches itself. The `java.lang.System` class is initialized in order to access its `out` field, and a Java string is printed. Finally, the thread is detached from the runtime once it has finished making Java calls. Everything is wrapped with a try/catch block to provide a default handler for any uncaught exceptions.

The example can be compiled with `c++ -c test.cc; gcj test.o`.

```
// test.cc
#include <gcj/cni.h>
#include <java/lang/System.h>
#include <java/io/PrintStream.h>
#include <java/lang/Throwable.h>

int main(int argc, char *argv[])
{
  using namespace java::lang;

  try
  {
    JvCreateJavaVM(NULL);
    JvAttachCurrentThread(NULL, NULL);

    String *message = JvNewStringLatin1("Hello from C++");
    JvInitClass(&System::class$);
    System::out->println(message);

    JvDetachCurrentThread();
  }
  catch (Throwable *t)
  {
    System::err->println(JvNewStringLatin1("Unhandled Java exception:"));
    t->printStackTrace();
  }
}
```

11.17 Reflection

Reflection is possible with CNI code, it functions similarly to how it functions with JNI.

The types `jfieldID` and `jmethodID` are as in JNI.

The functions:

- JvFromReflectedField,
- JvFromReflectedMethod,
- JvToReflectedField
- JvToFromReflectedMethod

will be added shortly, as will other functions corresponding to JNI.

12 System properties

The runtime behavior of the `libgcj` library can be modified by setting certain system properties. These properties can be compiled into the program using the `-Dname[=value]` option to `gcj` or by setting them explicitly in the program by calling the `java.lang.System.setProperty()` method. Some system properties are only used for informational purposes (like giving a version number or a user name). A program can inspect the current value of a property by calling the `java.lang.System.getProperty()` method.

12.1 Standard Properties

The following properties are normally found in all implementations of the core libraries for the Java language.

`java.version`

> The `libgcj` version number.

`java.vendor`

> Set to 'The Free Software Foundation, Inc.'

`java.vendor.url`

> Set to http://gcc.gnu.org/java/.

`java.home`

> The directory where `gcj` was installed. Taken from the `--prefix` option given to `configure`.

`java.class.version`

> The class format version number supported by the libgcj byte code interpreter. (Currently '46.0')

`java.vm.specification.version`

> The Virtual Machine Specification version implemented by `libgcj`. (Currently '1.0')

`java.vm.specification.vendor`

> The name of the Virtual Machine specification designer.

`java.vm.specification.name`

> The name of the Virtual Machine specification (Set to 'Java Virtual Machine Specification').

`java.vm.version`

> The `gcj` version number.

`java.vm.vendor`

> Set to 'The Free Software Foundation, Inc.'

`java.vm.name`

> Set to 'GNU libgcj'.

`java.specification.version`

> The Runtime Environment specification version implemented by `libgcj`. (Currently set to '1.3')

`java.specification.vendor`
>The Runtime Environment specification designer.

`java.specification.name`
>The name of the Runtime Environment specification (Set to 'Java Platform API Specification').

`java.class.path`
>The paths (jar files, zip files and directories) used for finding class files.

`java.library.path`
>Directory path used for finding native libraries.

`java.io.tmpdir`
>The directory used to put temporary files in.

`java.compiler`
>Name of the Just In Time compiler to use by the byte code interpreter. Currently not used in `libgcj`.

`java.ext.dirs`
>Directories containing jar files with extra libraries. Will be used when resolving classes.

`java.protocol.handler.pkgs`
>A '|' separated list of package names that is used to find classes that implement handlers for `java.net.URL`.

`java.rmi.server.codebase`
>A list of URLs that is used by the `java.rmi.server.RMIClassLoader` to load classes from.

`jdbc.drivers`
>A list of class names that will be loaded by the `java.sql.DriverManager` when it starts up.

`file.separator`
>The separator used in when directories are included in a filename (normally '/' or '\').

`file.encoding`
>The default character encoding used when converting platform native files to Unicode (usually set to '8859_1').

`path.separator`
>The standard separator used when a string contains multiple paths (normally ':' or ';'), the string is usually not a valid character to use in normal directory names.)

`line.separator`
>The default line separator used on the platform (normally '\n', '\r' or a combination of those two characters).

`policy.provider`
>The class name used for the default policy provider returned by `java.security.Policy.getPolicy`.

user.name

> The name of the user running the program. Can be the full name, the login name or empty if unknown.

user.home

> The default directory to put user specific files in.

user.dir The current working directory from which the program was started.

user.language

> The default language as used by the `java.util.Locale` class.

user.region

> The default region as used by the `java.util.Local` class.

user.variant

> The default variant of the language and region local used.

user.timezone

> The default timezone as used by the `java.util.TimeZone` class.

os.name The operating system/kernel name that the program runs on.

os.arch The hardware that we are running on.

os.version

> The version number of the operating system/kernel.

awt.appletWarning

> The string to display when an untrusted applet is displayed. Returned by `java.awt.Window.getWarningString()` when the window is "insecure".

awt.toolkit

> The class name used for initializing the default `java.awt.Toolkit`. Defaults to `gnu.awt.gtk.GtkToolkit`.

http.proxyHost

> Name of proxy host for http connections.

http.proxyPort

> Port number to use when a proxy host is in use.

12.2 GNU Classpath Properties

`libgcj` is based on the GNU Classpath (Essential Libraries for Java) a GNU project to create free core class libraries for use with virtual machines and compilers for the Java language. The following properties are common to libraries based on GNU Classpath.

gcj.dumpobject

> Enables printing serialization debugging by the `java.io.ObjectInput` and `java.io.ObjectOutput` classes when set to something else then the empty string. Only used when running a debug build of the library.

gnu.classpath.vm.shortname

> This is a succinct name of the virtual machine. For `libgcj`, this will always be 'libgcj'.

`gnu.classpath.home.url`
> A base URL used for finding system property files (e.g., 'classpath.security').∎
> By default this is a 'file:' URL pointing to the 'lib' directory under
> 'java.home'.

12.3 libgcj Runtime Properties

The following properties are specific to the `libgcj` runtime and will normally not be found
in other core libraries for the java language.

`java.fullversion`
> The combination of `java.vm.name` and `java.vm.version`.

`java.vm.info`
> Same as `java.fullversion`.

`impl.prefix`
> Used by the `java.net.DatagramSocket` class when set to something else then
> the empty string. When set all newly created `DatagramSocket`s will try to load
> a class `java.net.[impl.prefix]DatagramSocketImpl` instead of the normal
> `java.net.PlainDatagramSocketImpl`.

`gnu.gcj.progname`
> The class or binary name that was used to invoke the program. This will be
> the name of the "main" class in the case where the `gij` front end is used, or the
> program binary name in the case where an application is compiled to a native
> binary.

`gnu.gcj.user.realname`
> The real name of the user, as taken from the password file. This may not always
> hold only the user's name (as some sites put extra information in this field).
> Also, this property is not available on all platforms.

`gnu.gcj.runtime.NameFinder.use_addr2line`
> Whether an external process, `addr2line`, should be used to determine line num-
> ber information when tracing the stack. Setting this to `false` may suppress
> line numbers when printing stack traces and when using the java.util.logging in-
> frastructure. However, performance may improve significantly for applications
> that print stack traces or make logging calls frequently.

`gnu.gcj.runtime.NameFinder.show_raw`
> Whether the address of a stack frame should be printed when the line number
> is unavailable. Setting this to `true` will cause the name of the object and the
> offset within that object to be printed when no line number is available. This
> allows for off-line decoding of stack traces if necessary debug information is
> available. The default is `false`, no raw addresses are printed.

`gnu.gcj.runtime.NameFinder.remove_unknown`
> Whether stack frames for non-java code should be included in a stack trace. The
> default value is `true`, stack frames for non-java code are suppressed. Setting
> this to `false` will cause any non-java stack frames to be printed in addition to
> frames for the java code.

`gnu.gcj.runtime.VMClassLoader.library_control`

> This controls how shared libraries are automatically loaded by the built-in class loader. If this property is set to 'full', a full search is done for each requested class. If this property is set to 'cache', then any failed lookups are cached and not tried again. If this property is set to 'never' (the default), then lookups are never done. For more information, See Section 2.2 [Extensions], page 28.

`gnu.gcj.runtime.endorsed.dirs`

> This is like the standard `java.endorsed.dirs`, property, but specifies some extra directories which are searched after the standard endorsed directories. This is primarily useful for telling `libgcj` about additional libraries which are ordinarily incorporated into the JDK, and which should be loaded by the bootstrap class loader, but which are not yet part of `libgcj` itself for some reason.

`gnu.gcj.jit.compiler`

> This is the full path to `gcj` executable which should be used to compile classes just-in-time when `ClassLoader.defineClass` is called. If not set, `gcj` will not be invoked by the runtime; this can also be controlled via `Compiler.disable`.

`gnu.gcj.jit.options`

> This is a space-separated string of options which should be passed to `gcj` when in JIT mode. If not set, a sensible default is chosen.

`gnu.gcj.jit.cachedir`

> This is the directory where cached shared library files are stored. If not set, JIT compilation is disabled. This should never be set to a directory that is writable by any other user.

`gnu.gcj.precompiled.db.path`

> This is a sequence of file names, each referring to a file created by `gcj-dbtool`. These files will be used by `libgcj` to find shared libraries corresponding to classes that are loaded from bytecode. `libgcj` often has a built-in default database; it can be queried using `gcj-dbtool -p`.

13 Resources

While writing `gcj` and `libgcj` we have, of course, relied heavily on documentation from Sun Microsystems. In particular we have used The Java Language Specification (both first and second editions), the Java Class Libraries (volumes one and two), and the Java Virtual Machine Specification. In addition we've used Sun's online documentation.

The current `gcj` home page is `http://gcc.gnu.org/java/`.

For more information on GCC, see `http://gcc.gnu.org/`.

Some `libgcj` testing is done using the Mauve test suite. This is a free software Java class library test suite which is being written because the JCK is not free. See `http://www.sourceware.org/mauve/` for more information.

Index